The Valleys Are So Lush and Steep

TRACE PETERSON

saturnalia | BOOKS

Distributed by Independent Publishers Group
Chicago

©2025 Trace Peterson

No part of this book may be used or reproduced in any manner without written permission except in the case of brief quotations embodied in critical articles and reviews. Please direct inquiries to:

Saturnalia Books
2816 North Kent Rd.
Broomall, PA 19008
info@saturnaliabooks.com

ISBN: 978-1-9478178-83 (print), 978-1-9478178-90 (ebook)
Library of Congress Control Number: 2025938305

Cover art and book design by Robin Vuchnich

Distributed by:
Independent Publishing Group
814 N. Franklin St.
Chicago, IL 60610
800-888-4741

CONTENTS

AFTER BEFORE AND AFTER	3
THE VALLEYS ARE SO LUSH AND STEEP	5
THE VAST CROWD	15
NO ONE COULD SEE THE VAST CROWD	17
EVERYONE IS A LITTLE TRANS	20
IDENTIFICATION	27
THE OTHER MEMBERS WITH MY ID	36
VIOLET SPEECH	47
VIOLET SPEECH	49
CODA	69
VENUS	73
EXCLUSIVELY ON VENUS	75
CANYON OF HEROINES	77
PUSSY	79
MAKE A WISH	81
PERMANENTLY	86

EXPERIMENTAL LIFE	89
QUEER POEM	91
THE BAROMETER IN MY NECK	94
BOBADYLLO*	96
WIG CAP	97
BERLIN	98
MOVEABLE TYPE	99
THE BLUR	101
BOUQUET	103
HYDRO-POWERED TURBINES	104
NOCTURNE	105
DRONES	106
WITH A PETROLEUM COATING	107
WALKING UP TO THE PUNCHBOWL AS IF YOU OWN IT	108
ACKNOWLEDGEMENTS	111
ABOUT TRACE PETERSON	114

AFTER BEFORE AND AFTER

I've been freed from
inside the Fall of Rome,
my contract disrupted.
Civilization will
not descend without
my bet against it rising,
a weather balloon
that hangs against a vast
usurped sky. A carrier
pigeon, to be,
carries me. And from here
I can find the edge
of the cunning, supposedly
clear window that
divides us from the World
of Michael Kors, that
divides a kiss from
its aftertaste.
A coda is a beginning.
After before and
after, humane enclosures
air whips through
with a taste for blood
oranges and secret
unpoliced

temporal lace
have been spread out
imagining possible
goddesses in
bed. What's free
about a woman's stubble,
what's enhanced
delivering an urgent note
across a field of blue.

THE VALLEYS ARE SO LUSH AND STEEP

I have not been having an easy HRT experience for a trans gal, especially when it comes to blocking testosterone so my body can develop properly in response to estrogen.

*

Spironolactone gave me brain fog, so to block T, I switched to Finasteride.

*

The blocker dose of Finasteride made me too sleepy to function, so I switched to Progesterone.

*

Progesterone had some nice effects but it made me loopy and had a kind of thought-freezing quality, so I switched to Dutasteride.

*

Dutasteride made me too sleepy to function and caused me to phase shift into a fourth dimension at unexpected moments, so I switched to Walzanone.

*

Walzanone helped ease off my body hair, but it gave me unanticipated telekinetic powers which would cause a table to fly crashing across the room when I got upset with someone, so I switched to Benefiontin.

*

Benefiontin seemed to be working for a while and I could genuinely concentrate, until I slowly became aware that it was making my skin fluorescent green and stretchable over any nearby hardwood surfaces. Punk rock anamorphosis had ended long ago, so I switched to Penalzombion.

*

While I enjoyed the ultra-feminine high that Penalzombion enfaulked from my kinesthetic being, it had the unfortunate side effect of causing me to hate most poetry I hear, or maybe that was just poetry. In any case, the constant sore throat or what they call the "Penalzombion engorgement" became highly inconvenient when I needed to sing impromptu arias for job talks on composition theory. So I switched to Rubicon.

*

Though not technically a blocker, Rubicon had several advantages in terms of how it personified and mirrored my t-levels internally. A short-range tactical missile flew by in search of its drone-targeted recipient. Testosterone self-reflectiveness on Rubicon invaded my being on a coding level of intensity to the point where rows of shark teeth swallowed every time management skill I ever learned. There was no going back. I decided that Rubicon was too much of a simultaneously alienated and intimately ski mask experience. So I switched to Novascotia.

*

The best side effect of Novascotia was its remoteness. Though it made me feel slightly alienated around other poets, I did manage to get a lot of writing done. However, in the process I lost all sense of reality and missed my grant deadlines for the fourth time. A mouse ear grew out of my hand. Peach cobbler. So I switched to Nepotismapolitan.

*

With Nepotismapolitan I definitely engrotted some anti-testosterone connections in the entertainment world, which had me at an advantage when passing as entertainmentally female, but my pores became enormous. When I think back I wonder if Nepotismapolitan was taunting me the whole time. Gam tumescent wing growth polited out of the sinking vessel. Due to interaction warnings I couldn't eat too much processed food anymore and my T levels were still too high, so I switched to Wellmasteride.

*

I liked the feeling of cosmic omnipotence corresponding with complete and utter abjection that Wellmasteride gave me, being at once a unique delicate flower/snowflake and a humanistic reproconfection seeking air time like every other platelet in the bloodstream, but it made me leery of discussions about trigger warnings and delaying puberty in children. Pang of detained weekend fixture turned permanent yawp. I stopped thugging around in my endocrine blotter with Wellmasteride, and instead turned to Jamieleecurtisol.

*

Jamieleecurtisol made me witty and urbane. Being around me was like an episode of female Frasier slightly sped up. But soon the crash happened and we were in a recession. Jamieleecurtisol caused me to scream and scream at the horrible truth about how people really perceived my gender suddenly rushing at me around street corners. So I switched to Smallpondilaxone.

*

Smallpondilaxone made me feel big.

For a minute I contemplated calling an agent

to discuss my enormous very specialized coupon stash, but I

couldn't get out of bed. So next I tried Crepusculane.

*

Now the great thing about Crepusculane was that on this one I really felt like myself on five cups of coffee for a few minutes lugging a trampoline up the capitol steps past the stone lions that guarded the secret to what's inside increasingly smaller panties I never held any responsibility for, a good place to do research. I made all kinds of appointments to publish poet things and attend everybody's readings in a stacker, almost steroid-like configuration demented with charm. But the hyper-concentration that Crepusculane offers caused me instead to stare at a Grecian Urn for days on end, transfixed by thoughts of lighting up and smoking the latest poet laureate or at least getting a medical prescription for him/her to become culturally all over me. Crepusculane rendered my t-levels nearly invisible as I lay swooning across a Chatterton velvet couch in my garret, but there was no one around but me to serenade, so I switched to Lesbiamine.

*

Lesbiamine caused ………………………………………….. in peace talks ………..
…………………………………………………………………………………………….
…………………………....…………... rankled tall girl spat juicer ………………….. but
…………………………………………………………………………………………….
………………. looks at your spork ……………………... like a gorgon, tufts of ……..
……………………………………………………..…………………………………….
kissing us in the museum ……………………………………………………...………..
………………………………….…… making me ……………. attachment weekend blocker.
…………………………………………………………………………………………….
my leg around your …………………………………………………………………...
………………………………………... wetter, a death ……..……………….. bank holiday itch...
………………………………………………………………………………………….....
clasped ……………………………………………….. in a restaurant booth …………….....
……..or vamp stamped ……………………….. something chocolate …………………..……..
…………………………………………………………………………………………….
…………...……………………..anxiety being unsexy…………………………………….
…………….and you need lateness ……………………………………………………..
destorying me ……………………………………………………………………………..
………………..………………………………………….too intense………………………..

like the crushed flower. I couldn't take all the ellipses anymore and they were intruding into my dissertation writing time, so I switched to Pastoralwenchtrin.

*

I think I am going to stick with Pastoralwenchtrin for a while and see where this goes. It's quiet here and there are sheep and no wolves masquerading as bears climbing the hillside of an apple danish I bought from my student loan debt ceiling. Ah ah, woo hoo yeah. As long as I pay the credit card bills by end of the month and get my name changed in time for the church basement sale, maybe I can find a way to live.

As my body reaches a kind of equilibrium, I am trying to have as small a percentage of me as possible be fabricated as method acting and as great a possibility as a pink skull half-shaven skyline be real.

The valleys are so lush and steep.

How to end not wanting to be myself being not quite myself.

THE VAST CROWD

NO ONE COULD SEE THE VAST CROWD

This is a working sentence.
Someone walks by.
Three sentences standing around bonding.
Terrible, terrible sentences.
The third sentence resents the fourth sentence more than the fifth.
Sitting in a late cafe crying.
Trying to stare down carbs with the mistress's tools.
A panoply of belated newsprint.
A drain stopper with a dripping faucet.
Coming in and coming out of the same entrance marked urgent.
Paragraphs concealing whole illegal phrases.
You marked me like this.
Your flesh was a styrofoam packing glitch.
My flesh was plastic rotary phone alimony.
I carried about you into my term limits.
No one could see the vast crowd.
Is my protection really there.
Is my storm drain a liar, I said, a lair.
If you can hear the sound of my voice.
If you can weep.
Who seek the quiet non-quiet ingénue
showing up with an awareness strapped to her back
and frills, and seasonless outhouse-amending night.
If you can swallow a horse pill.
If you can correct the record so it

flips closed. If you can barrel through the legislation
with a fringe. Pages and pages
betray one another on a whim.
Stand up to the breaker maybe.
The surface is grime. The spandrels
a delicate balance. The fasces
that made our avarice great.
They entrap a womb to leverage mani-pedi channels
Actually, I don't have a mani-pedi lack.
Resistance comes back.
The tumbling locrian meathouse of our maker
our grower, our pretender.
Very very very very very very.
To flatten out the stomach acid.
To paint the birds closed.
A public forest of intangible treeless forms
applauding their ascension. The recycle
bin moves me to tears like a
second chance for ampersand hearts.
A lariat and a missile shield.
What is this poem really about, Trace? Well,
last week you died. You did.
Everything was getting so concrete.
I didn't know you were going to leave
and the medium was keeping us apart.

A panoply of belated newsprint.
Sitting in a late cafe crying.
I discover just as you have become
a signal rushing through a wire signing off.
People are not words or sentences.
I hate social media. You were so
positive and I argued back continually.
If the floor pulled out with each new
memory blaming a distraction.
How many more will die. When does
the surrealism dry up completely.
If you can hear the sound of my voice
tonight I'm at a protest march in the cold.
In socialist realist syntax I am shouting
up at a distant apartment window trying
to provoke any action from a
complacent person in power.

EVERYONE IS A LITTLE TRANS

Everyone is a little Trans
Everyone is a little Bisexual
Everyone is a little Genderqueer
Everyone is a little Not There

Everyone is a little Enby
Everyone is a little Gender Fluid
Everyone is a little twelve inch pianist
Everyone is a little Cis

Everyone is a little circular rubbing motion
Everyone thinks they're Billy Ocean

Everyone is a forgotten hit record
Everyone is a little good at sex
Everyone is a little bad at gender

Everyone is a little changeable
Everyone is a little rigidly stuck in their thing
Everyone is a Post Office Worker
Everyone is an abandoned carousel with empty horses going around and around and around

Everyone is a little lurker
Everyone is a little mako shark
Everyone is a little romper wearing narc
Everyone is a little tailor with a broadcloth under zir arm

Everyone is a little stitch in time
Everyone is a little grammatical error that changed the meaning of our relationship completely by accidentally introducing a surprise microaggression
Everyone is a little discriminated against
Everyone is a little interested in sitting on the dryer while it vibrates

Everyone tells us everyone is a little gay means everyone who is cis
Everyone is a little white crisply ironed shirt
Everyone is a poet
Everyone says no more than what they meant

Everyone has disappeared from sight
Everyone is a little missing
Everyone is a little ventriloquized by this puppet
Everyone farts with zir armpit

Everyone is a little scientist building rockets
Everyone says it's not rocket science even when it is
Everyone is an ineffective gangster
Everyone is camped out waiting on the grass for Shakespeare in the Park tickets

Everyone is a little unspecific thing
Everyone is a spork
Everyone is a precise floating ethereal ectoplasm except when it's time to pick up a paycheck or eat or have sex or clean the bathroom or get attacked on the street for just existing

Everyone is a little angry
Everyone is getting on my last nerve
Everyone has poor food truck boundaries
Everyone shows a complete lack of respect for lack

Everyone is a little ignorant of how much better they have it than everyone
Everyone is a method actor
Everyone is a monster

Everyone drives a tractor
Everyone provides a blank member
Everyone listens to thrash metal
Everyone guesses the lottery number correctly

Everyone wins!
Everyone is a little newt
Everyone collapses into parallel dimensions when they hear a Broadway musical begin

Everyone is now a little stand offish
Everyone is better than everyone else
Everyone is enjoying being penetrated
Everyone by stunning realizations and ideas from the history of western thought

Everyone is a little tired of liberal arts and its oppressive regime
Everyone is a little academically non conforming
Everyone is a little ADD
Everyone is me

Everyone is a little hog tied
Everyone is a little burbling brook
Everyone ditched their nook
Everyone is a little more into buying things online now to save trees from certain destruction even though global warming doesn't officially exist

Everyone is a little smarter
Everyone is a little taller because of all the preservatives
Everyone is a little prepackaged
Everyone is wreckage

IDENTIFICATION

"Can I see your ID?"

"Here it is. I changed my sex so I don't look like this anymore, but you get the idea."

"Can I see your ID?"

"No."

"Can I see your ID?"

"You may, but in the end isn't disidentification really the more important discursive move?"

"Can I see your ID?"

"Oh, Balzac."

*

"Can I see your ID?"

"I pledge allegiance to the flag of the United States of America."

"Can I see your ID?"

"Gross."

"Can I see your ID?"

"Do I really need an ID to return something that I already have a receipt for?"

"Can I see your ID?"

"Oh you know, like Candy Darling but female."

*

"Can I see your ID?"

"Well I guess the bigger question might be, is the ID really there?"

"Can I see your ID?"

"Drew Barrymore meets Jamie Lee Curtis meets Poison Ivy."

*

"Can I see your ID?"

"No "

"Can I see your ID?"

"NOT READY TO ARM"

"Can I see your ID?"

"Well ok but the ID I am about to show you does not look anything like me. See, I got into a bizarre disfiguring accident with several smug, popular schools of academic theory."

*

"Can I see your ID?"

"I on honeydew hath fed and drunk the milk of paradise."

"Can I see your ID?"

"That depends."

"Can I see your ID?"

"Hey, you're a different guy from the last time I shopped here."

"Can I see your ID?"

"Have you ever heard of a little something called Neoplatonism?

*

"Can I see your ID?"

"Can I see your T'ai Chi?"

"Can I see your ID?"

"Yes, just close your eyes…now think of fairies and pixie dust."

*

"Can I see your ID?"

"Yes and No."

"Can I see your ID?"

"I have one of those new nano IDs actually and I am not sure which of these inarticulate clumps of detritus it is hiding among in my purse. Would you like to help me look?"

"Can I see your ID?"

"Yes, I agree that a vagina is the most transcendent possible thing to have."

*

"Can I see your ID?"

"Yes, if you can answer this riddle! What walks on four legs in the morning, two legs right now during her lunch break, and three legs in the evening?"

"Can I see your ID?"

"Oh, you know like Imogen Binnie but short and bespectacled and writes poetry."

*

"Can I see your ID?"

"I now declare myself to be Trace."

"Can I see your ID?"

"Here you go. Is it possible to change the name on this ID? Oh, I just call this number here and speak with a customer representative?"

*

"Can I see your ID?"

"You can, but a woman's ID is printed in the wind and running water."

"Can I see your ID?"

"I'm rubber, you're glue."

"Can I see your ID?"

"My IUD? Yes you can totally see that."

"Can I see your ID?"

"Why don't you light a few more candles, and maybe I can get in the mood."

*

"Can I see your ID?"

"And I would have succeeded with my evil plan too, if it hadn't been for you lousy kids!"

"Can I see your ID?"

"What, my *meatspace* ID?"

"Can I see your ID?"

"Troelstrup nightmare risen, quiz motivation tincture reality."

"Can I see your ID?"

"Oh you know, like Laverne Cox but the Swedish/French WASP version."

*

"Can I see your ID?"

"So here's the deal, you correctly called me ma'am a second ago but now I am going to have to ask you to go against all available legal evidence and ask you to continue calling me ma'am after you have seen it."

"Can I see your ID?"

"Shit fuck piss cocker puss cunt waco dominant fallopian gyno-bot womp decal mother trucker wall detroit czechoslovakia dromedary fuckhouse."

"Can I see your ID?"

"I don't know, *can* you?"

THE OTHER MEMBERS WITH MY ID

The seedy motel in
Manchester has installed
mirrors above the beds.
I forget how we know that.
A neighbor has maybe
gossiped around the pool
I almost drown in.
Maybe it's *True Blue*,
looking on as my first
girlfriend performs a dance
routine for the other family,
unrolling a long silk
opera glove. I listen timidly
tim timer tremor trailer
tryouts tricycle to
tremble jealously. A gal
from a small town like me
still in previews. My parents
protest war-games. I
listen on my best friend's
sister Aviva's headphones
to *True Colors*. Who and who.

*

Let me critique what
I'm saying about the other
members with my ID.
Apparently the first time
I desired anything I
stayed up all night
thinking about its name
in coalescing form.
A library window
splashed with light. Outside
Three men all in white
hoods with eyeholes cut
out of them march along
Main Street. Three too many.
Pathetic, their thick robes
drag on the ground. My
father says "Oh, they're
really bad, they're evil." I
must tell you I forget
how we know that too. Across
the street, a bronze-blue
Union soldier looks away.

*

Who is writing this now,
nurtured in a garden of
intertwined abandon? Branch,
support emoji, wings flap.
Who left the apples out
with goddess statues on
the lawn? I had no
choice but to wake from it.
If the ampersand arena
discernment and pleasure
in which I wound myself
falls away what is there.
I guess it's *you*? The walls
are chalk white! Some dude
grabs my hand to avoid
floating away like space
junk into the atmosphere.
I give and give. He'll love me
burning up rapidly on
re-entry and become me.

*

Somebody laid out the cosmos
interspersed with dahlias and
phlox, we tell ourselves as
long as we can identify their
names. The wrong God
shifts my file folder back
in the drawer.   *I made this
whole place so she couldn't
exist.*   *He made this
whole place so I couldn't
exist.*   Cradling my anger.
Here's a weak point in the cage
we thought we built.
Tear it down to the asphalt.

*

Today the grass of childhood
smells alarming and freshly
cut. I'm obsessed by its
loneliness, how it enlists
yard work in becoming itself
reading about the real in a
violent news video. Everyone
is feeling a certain way
about Bob Dylan. Everyone
is signing a contract for a split
level reality series: childhood
and everything that murders it.
Carlos climbs the jungle gym
beside me. I love him.
The entire sky blinks red.
Suffering underlies the
town like a grid, kissing
hysteria in a graveyard
of unmarked names.

*

It falls to us. A splintered
desire dissolves and
we cross the street. This
is my ID. I'm not like the rest,
I'm *me*. Don't you want to check
my *status*? I am the only
queer person at your party, face
pressed against chilled glass.
I am the only white
person at another party
because we're flipping the context
because of all the mummies
that stay dead enclosing me
from all sides in full
stolen regalia. I try to speak
through this bandage across a
bridge above the roiling blue.

*

That's not a life. I transfer
leaving an impression. My co-author's
face is a washcloth wrung out
with thoughts of being unsafe
or exposed by a mechanism
like a forbidden apple without
a core. You got here and
it's too late now for food,
the kitchen closed an hour
ago. O the alienated hearts
hearts hearts hearts you got here
and found your would-be lover
stockpiling guns. Sign on
the house says "You
Matter" in a Black Lives
Matter font. Anagnorisis
baits. The next line unfolds,
pulling a comb through the lice,
becoming a tattered voice
that protests in the street
the last time this happened.
The last time this happened
to the popular vote, we

float over the abandoned
context like a god's face
moving above the raging blue.

*

The gravy boat forms a skin.
Acres of people with
my nose, growing corn
claim to see through me, but
that's *my* superpower. Their
silken silhouettes dance
against the bonfire of a
nightmare I can't wake. Blue-
grass plays in the background.
Smoke from books and limbs
triggers an alarm I don't
want to not feel alone.
Half the labor is inaccessible
and from home. I have moved
his heart into my chest.
I am flowing into his time.
Tonight we protest

fascist creep on 42nd street,
before the other members
can steal our rage. A line
of police has surrounded us
and is advancing screeching
Please disperse or you
will be arrested and sent
to a men's prison. They press
forward. That's not my life too.
Behind the crowd my friend, you
find a hidden door into a
building somewhere behind the
barrier. The handle moves.
And we may never pass
but we slip through.

VIOLET SPEECH

VIOLET SPEECH

The violets in the mixed perennial border, plump, with lacy edges, come in a variety of purples.

The violets providing orally answered please rise please stand.

The undertenant of said premises, stem to petiole to leaf, voiced several stipulations drooping after rain, sweet craolo vortex stain.

A cross-examination: How do you answer the stigma style petal ovary?

I speak an unlisted option, stigma anther.
                                                                                An argument ensues

and I'm insisting, now shouting at the clerk behind the desk. Like a buzzing bee he gathers drones, hardons.

I am his receptacle, discretion.

Perennial violets spread by creeping roots and rhizomes, duly sworn before a plaque that reads "In God We Trust."

The entire garden bed, a court, a caption for that plaque we saw behind the violet's head, low-slung ceilings miracle-gro, cheap nametag font cotyledens.

TAKE NOTICE, the court has decided:

Violet speech is harmful.

Violet speech cannot be legislated.

The violet we'd want eluded its propositioner's desires, this field too dark fuchsia, this malevolent light purple body too foregoing to surrender up sun rays.

Armies recline on armoires, illuminated by the occasional flash of violet color. Gray resentful faces walk among violets marred by an amendment by the claimant.

Words hammered at the dais around which violets gathered, clamoring for restrictions on our need to legislate the fact that we were violets were conscious of what was said about us, how we avoided becoming a plot that could be quantified, surrounded, dug up.

Stigma style petal ovary

How we approach the bench, bed

Violets caption hammered

                                          Armies

Font cotyledons flash please rise

We avoided, marred   Gathers drones

Self-pollinated, donning a not

A meadow discontinuance open

Need this threatened   Bractaeoles

Donning a swarming

The dirt is swarming with small-flowered hybrid lawyers. A violet donning a suit, suit donning a violet, I pray for a meadow discontinuance up close.

Instead I get an untitled judgment: dismissal without prejudice, like the painter Rothko. A line composed of complementary colors divides the bracteoles of the canvas in the proportions of a figure with vibrating edges. A human figure, not a violet, self-pollinated and pointing downward, thinks thickets. The entire garden bed a court, the family ranging from nutlike seeds spread by ants stalking the sheets, but violets are not as powerful as passive resistance.

Outside, I breathe in the purple air, a woman observes my violet suit stops me and asks if I'm here for the beer-tasting meetup. After blooming, we visit the Metropolitan Museum and pay the minimum endosperm fee. After blooming, we produce capsules that when they open grow into poems.

Rothko dismissal ranging passive

Violet day publicly blooming

Breathe in the endosperm

Receptacle asks when they open

                                                              Grow

Among instead   Sponsor, higher power

I pray red square backing

                                              Modeling

Rothko boxes dead heads

Liminal early lagging   Fade listening

Dilapidated amendment

                            Array

But back to what I was saying about Rothko's paintings. Rothko sits through the entire self-help session listening to everyone talk, then when he opens his mouth about four people, all violets, get up and leave.

Rothko is extremely upset, purple, blue, yellow, and so am I. It makes him feel his paintings aren't worth listening to. They actually barely are, barely there, confronted instead by the human form already segmented like a coffin, cut to abstract proportions of a dead head. Most painters lose their attraction as they fade, although some argue that dead heading can increase performance.

I'd complain about this simplification to the dark red square taking up the bottom corner, as if it could remember former blooms.

If the boxes shtick gets old and the rules underlying them change, like natural selection, would hurt adapt? Would the ability to be art?

Rothko attempts to answer me here using terms like "sponsor" and "higher power," but his liminal early canvases speak otherwise. I am lagging behind the group now, looking them over.

Is Rothko a petitioner, a respondent, or a lawyer?
                                             Am I Rothko?

Repetition isn't inevitable, the demon who suddenly appears to you in the poem and says "you are doomed to always write about violets." Instead you can make an atmospheric scene of a subway like Rothko did, with a dour glowing color combination that creates depth within a shallow space, reaching around like a body that belies available discourse.

I notice something flash on the street outside, something violet. I try to take a photo out the window.

Argue segmented Rothko

Embodied life   Dour phrase factory

Coffin respondent a violet

Spring impinges

                                    Self-help tragic

Lagging poem belies you'd point

Strategic layout   Running water

Canvases otherwise petitioner

Barely a shallow

At this stage, total estimate for poem construction is $92,800 plus tax. Installation of the Rothko paintings may cost extra due to shipping-related precautions. Importation of specific breeds of violets adds possible embodied energy, with additional costs anticipated for continued maintenance as spring impinges on us, opening the poem like a bloom that only appears fictitious.

In order to proceed, we need to have 30 percent of the allegory provided up front. We look forward to working with you and helping you take your poem to the next level, loosening up that frame which could have doomed you to a tragic metaphor: Orpheus, Electra, Pandora, et al. Once the initial design phase has been completed, installation of poem on stainless steel or concrete requires an additional two months but installation on wind and running water is negligible.

Strategic alternation of metaphors of artistic genius and altruistic service allows us to speak through you, actually providing impetus for the poems but not, you'd argue, making the real *design decisions*. Have you been subordinated to the engineering process at this point, your you being written like an accident? Are you a factory poet? As long as you contribute an appropriately large deposit up front, we won't need to answer that question.

Sincerely,

War of the Worlds Design Systems.

Contribute to unhappiness   Up

Due to lack   Shipping-related

Fourteen blocks of tragic your you

Lace-topped challenge   Accident

We need continued Rothko terminals

Made of saliva
                    Lack fibers

Working for antennae to proceed

Open-plan spring a nest

Appears rearing prefer
                              Hunched dreamily

It's a challenge working for the wasps, hunched secretly among them at endless computer terminals made of paper fibers collected from dry wood, bark, and saliva, googling away. Or do they work for me and my shifting boundaries? The wasps rely on a nest from which we conduct many activities: rearing young, installing fourteen blocks of new housing, accentuating the open-plan layout of very low lace-topped necks. When they order me to "get on top of things" in wasp language, communicated by saliva collusion antennae collision, I need to remind myself: these males lack a stinger.

A reluctant wasp, I prefer instead to stare out the L-shaped sky patios dreamily on a softly padded, observe orientation take advantage of the sun, how they stage thrills an overlapping of program and landscape elements, various periods of extreme tight-lacing. I accumulate this and other strings of words for the wasps as a means of translating their desires. Maybe they won't notice the violet streaks.

Cutting our teeth on competition wins, highly varied commissions, and the life-juices of potent younger firms, we typically build our umbrella-shaped nests under eaves and ledges. But wasp waist laces stick, tightly drawn in, abate, distrust my fag-brain description of the hives we slenderly experience, buttoned up to promote biodiversity.

Altruistic service a saliva

Slenderly fag-brain competition

Other insect hardened by hole

Landscape patron   Morally smug

Wing cutaway sort of day

I could remove   Private roofs

Cyberspace tendons

                         Fuck face

Punctured in a lower loss

Breathed openly integrated

Slenderly than mere away

TAKE NOTICE: If you fail to answer or appear, the wasps won't reveal the secrets of our real parasitic or predaceous activities which play a vital role in limiting the populations of other insect species. Yet sometimes I see a few of them through a crack in the combs, laying their eggs inside a client or vendor.

TAKE NOTICE: When the client appears puffed-up, brown, and hardened by typological research, the adult parasitic wasps chew a round hole in the abdomen to emerge. When I see this behavior it still turns my stomach, and I almost want to put down the caterpillar the throat of which I'm currently sucking the juice from.

The wasps, like Rothko, are *nice modernists*.

Nice laying vital   Play client

Focus ornamenting a draft

Volatile turns my brain my spine

Caterpillar team   Green rug

Porticos chagrin appears client

Almost want the wasp pathos

Design team hardened
                              Adult still

Zooming back to reveal

Identity is so messy, like an essay. Can this escape from legislation be legislated? I'm starting to distrust myself as a client, I thought, so I'll get on top of things. I'll try to see how many components I can remove, uncover the essence.

First the wasp waist goes into the dumpster, then the wasp pathos, then the contours of my face, rudimentary projecting cornice. My left arm, at the spot where it enters the torso (see longitudinal section) is detached for recycling and reuse in someone's trussed timber roof. I'm almost bare, a morally smug green rug. Almost there.

But when I discover I've thrown half my brain into cyberspace, I stage a protest against my design team, pensive violets ornamenting my loss. In effect, I'm dead heading my own chagrin. The arch of my spine, already punctured in a lower quadrant, falls into the next stanza on a grand scale (see cutaway elevation). A monster I breathe openly, without lungs, more integrated into the landscape than before, allowing for a sense of community that also includes spaces for private reflection. Like an open plan office pitched to the unsuspecting wasp, I predict production porticos.

Yet in private moments, of which there are now none, I keep zooming focus back to the bed of violets, poring over their legal briefs in long slow drafts that provoke the essence of volatile lived norms.

For example, some violets have a special shaped flower petal that resembles a wasp wing, but to draw this comparison would be like installing plants as one of your parents.

The leaves, it's true, looked like a bustle from an old-fashioned dress.

Equipment monster openly

Quadrant fell an Orpheus day

Application of stone to loss

Chagrin my spine

                                                     Old-fashioned

Without they them a smug see

Try to look heart-shaped

                                                     Bustle beetle

Punctured of reflection

                                                     My left

The petitioner prays for a final judgment of eviction, awarding to the petitioner possession of premises described as follows:

        Bed of violets

                            Writing subject

                                                    wasp nest

                Rothko

                            Political opinions

       Writer's body

                      Vision

                                      Reader

             Fingernails

                    Purse.

Who is the petitioner, the middle manager?

This cutaway section of the violet shows all the equipment you need to identify as kidney-shaped, heart-shaped, or actively growing.

This anther, it's true, contains a pollen cross-section which allows internal drainage.

The application of stone to the blossom, rather than mere cladding, creates an Orpheus sort of day in which

re-membered surface

constitutes functionality.

Well ok, so I'm stuck with a plaque that reads "In God We Trust" written in ten ugly fonts on the back wall. It doesn't move me at all.

Now approach the bench: a hunch, a group of wasps and the violets that try to look like them, or maybe they're violets and the wasps who try to be their them.

Try to look.

Who is writing this?

Fuck.

Suddenly a wasp (a violet?) lands on the Rothko painting and tries to suck it dry.

CODA

What used to be chivalrous is now unassertive.

What used to be charmingly self-deprecating is now painfully self-negating.

What used to be appreciated as supportive is now demanded and enforced at penalty of a heavy fine.

What used to be tender is now insultingly condescending.

What used to be considered a brilliant comment is now acceptable provided a nearby male approves it and agrees.

What used to be a witty conversational riposte is now aggressive or even violet.

What used to be shit doesn't stink.

What used to be intimacy is now sitting in the waiting room, a nicely decorated waiting room with flowers, wasps, piped-in smooth jazz, and terrible magazines.

What used to be terrifying is now harmless.

What used to be what used to be is now another person's life.

What used to be the complex development of a long, heroic Bildungsroman is now The Days of Our Lives meets Hot In Cleveland meets Alien.

What used to be an idle theory or idea is now showing up as the proof of my discourse, which changes what had been initially meant, that I am not in fact a discourse or a theory or an idea but someone other than those things.

What used to be self-consciousness is now the necessity to always remain alert.

What used to be basic kindness is now flirting.

What used to be rejection is now perky, veiled rejection.

What used to be poetry is now poetry.

What used to be expertise or knowledge or experience is a swarm of ambient words he barely hears looking deep into your peerless eyes.

What used to be humiliating is now strengthening, emboldening.

What used to be human is now reframeable.

What used to be water is now steam.

VENUS

EXCLUSIVELY ON VENUS

Roses are red / violets are transsexual / welcome to womanhood / now get to work honey

Roses are performative / violets are biological / I have very sensitive breasts / and so do your breasts

Roses are biological / you have the nicest skin / I can't stop kissing you / let's read more nondualistic queer theory

Roses are fed up / with our binary fetishes / I tricked my doctors / and stole all the medication to hide it in a cave and share it with other trans people

Roses have got me / up against the wall / kissing my neck / which is socially constructed to be a super hot strong feminist neck

Roses are violet / violets are roses / I really like you / I like you tube

Roses are born this way / violets have a lesbian streak / something about your dry sense of humor and our intertwined limbs / feels transcendently female

Roses are blue / violets are violet / roses are nonviolet / blue is bluenormative

Roses are from mars / violets had the whole surgery / setting up camp / exclusively on Venus

Roses have gone too far / not to be what girls are made of / I'm coming out / to my academic colleagues as a poet and I bet they will run away screaming

Roses are roses / violets are born this way / someone's got a hoard / of heteronormative transaffirmation porn you say?

Roses are cheeky / I want you to fuck me / drown violets like an accused witch / in your arms which feel like mine

Violets got a name change / roses changed a pronoun / we ate at a restaurant / and forgot to put the leftovers in the fridge

Roses are trochaic / violets have their original plumbing / let's march in a protest / then go home and we'll cook something delicious and eat it with a spork

Violets are permanent / roses are impermanent / thank you for becoming me / offering to embrace your form your fate

Flowerbeds are umbrellas / umbrellas are rubrics / I support your identification / and your disidentification

Men are from women / roses are from Jupiter / women are from men / I can't tell which is softer, your lips or this pillow or the snow descending gracefully outside

CANYON OF HEROINES

This bag of crunchy Cheetos is making me thirsty. Good thing I picked up a Fanta orange soda on the way home just in case. Walking back, I couldn't help noticing how most of the neighborhood has been replaced by strange towering steel and plate glass structures. A man was lying across the sidewalk in front of one of them and asked me for money. Greece is being bullied by Germany holding it to a double standard. When they had the tickertape parade for the US Women's Soccer Team this week and said "Canyon of Heroines" on the radio I started to laugh and realized it wasn't funny. The guy at an adjacent table in the coffee shop was looking at me smokily for an hour like he wanted to do something to me all over the counter, and I gave the possibility more consideration than I ever had before. I have trans woman friends who desperately need hope and jobs and love and safety and family. I wish I could be twenty places at once and have the power to fix everything but in a stealth way so I wouldn't be just grabbing the spotlight. True Detective is a TV show that a lot of people seem to enjoy. I trained myself to speak at a higher base pitch every morning until it became quasi-permanent because that is how I know I do not depend on the medical establishment or strangers' willingness to imagine charity. Much of the street is submerged underwater due to the storm. That other salesman can assist you--I'm helping this young lady right now, he said, placing his hand on the small of my back. The entire auditorium of people staring me down was hostile but knew they couldn't show it in public except for occasional frown lines darting from between their eyebrows. Please stand clear of the closing doors. I can't breathe in this dress. I can't seem to figure out where that smell is coming from in the apartment. Gender identity or expression will not protect you from being fired in most employment situations nor does being a transsexual woman. Split a capsule of medication into smaller doses by opening, dividing, and mixing it among separate containers of a mushy food like applesauce. The Trans-Pacific Partnership was signed this week amid much controversy. Did I just write all that? History is transmisogynistic but it won't be the more of it there is. The beautiful woman suggested I put my bare legs across her lap in the dark so I did and she gently ran her fingers along them. Wheat germ is where the problems all started. Later you asked if you could put your arm around me on the train but there was some scary guy shouting at everyone in the subway car and I didn't want to provoke him. People I love are at risk of being violently harmed or murdered every day, or they suffer from suicidal urges because of how the world fails to see us as people in a million sharp pointy little ways. Welcome to the military. The three-panel dressing room mirror had a Busby Berkeley effect which gave me a little thrill but I might have just imagined it. I wish I knew how to code things with boolean operators. I wish I knew how to read philosophy. The x-ray machine operator kept repeating "STOP BREATHING NOW DON'T BREATHE" each time he activated the machine. #CaitlynJenner

PUSSY

my butt
my back
my stomach
my breasts
my shoulders
my arms leaning on the table
my uncanny valley
my deskjob aversion
my porcupine quills
my stoppages
my filler
my quicksand
my elevated archness
my foolproof schemes
my childlessness
my shipping costs
my frozen Hopper characters huddled in a diner
my ballistics estimates coming in under budget
my hair falling all around my face
my blind spot
my blond spit
my softness
my blocked doorway
my insufficient "no"

my unfuckability

my team

my timing

my authorial deferment

my duplicate checks

my straining to see the others

my U-Haul following behind

my gait

my educating

my fogging up the window looking in on

my schooling

my pushing back adjacent to

my facts

MAKE A WISH

A million teaching moments

at our new location

is a monster with headless eyes

I shared to be kind. A dim

guitar weaves together bodies

that ossify. Mother's Day

provides evidence for our

argument that undoes it, my

animate hand caressing

the length of you. Who gets

to be an atmosphere, really,

her entire back covered with

rentals, a mating dance you can

feel shifting genders. Who

can stay gluten free under such

corrosive duress being poked

repeatedly in the same

bruised spot when liberal

desire conjures and slays

me? My sentences

disappear into you

like a snake waiting for an

echo, a forbidden fruit

canyon of lips, feet,

tendons, parasols, entire

voices declaring hardship

against a real girl. It's only

us reproducing the

dilated world of strollers

with stuck wheels reveling

in the April I gravel. The wasp

having deposited the mail

arguments waiting for

UPS endlessly. The bell

rings now. It's not for me.

It *is* for me! It's giving

mixed signals like a nape

to kiss a path along, wired

to a range of ghosts who

caress my name. You're

floating there, too. I love

you. And I disbelieve or can't

unsnarl my peace in a brightly lit

dinner party ringed with hurt

and a placemat offering

authorship that lasts.

PERMANENTLY

My audience falls away, but my audience gets stronger. I am not writing for anyone, but I am writing for you. I am simultaneously a solid a liquid and a gas and hue. My friends fade but my friends are everywhere and intimately real. No one is listening but everyone is listening. I am invisible but I am unavoidable. I am visible but I am a ghostbuster. My world got smaller but my environment got enormous. Awnings try to shade me but I slip by without stepping under them. This sentence has been erased but the sentence bled through and stained the garment permanently first. I am squeezed into a tiny container and I am too vast for you to see all of at once. I am a pectoral muscle and I am a breast. I cancelled my subscriptions but *Vogue* is still arriving monthly. My acronyms have multiple referents while moonlighting as neologisms. I am an ampersand and I am a pronoun. Parkas protect me from rain but I am the rain pouring over everyone. I am more serious than SRS. Cupcakes can just go ahead and eat me. Milloseconds of lust for a warm embrace into view I freeze. Pantsuits flee from my pantsuit. I am a woman and an opening of discourse petulance amphora kraken. I dilate but I concentrate. I emerge victorious having lost things unnoticed and unappreciated from the swamp of eminent domain. I pay the fee that I am too poor to pay. I climb the side of an idea that has a crush on my molten heart. I am a body trapped in a book that is a book trapped in a body. My pulse races through a low blood pressure front to yeast rising. This sentence is final as in completely incomplete. I am a swollen clit at an oblique angle to reality sparks of code. I am nobody but I am a body built by ignorance and refusal. I am somebody but the cloud opens and rains on cue. I am a sheep in wolf's clothing. My pen that cannot write keeps flowing ink from an empty impetus. My minimalist transverse intersection can beat up your honors student. I lick stamps without a tongue and send letters I will never mail. My enervated line dredges real opinion from the muck and slime. I exist and you may have imagined me. My feet sweat without a mermaid net. I am naturalistic and I am a stranger. My hips envelop this sentence as my torso twists toward your stormfront. I pulverize wholeness anticipating completeness. I am she whose parking spot is continually nabbed by a faster more unlikely car. I am irresistable and too many calories to consume in one sitting. Burned by the scorched earth policy, I grow back flame-retardant. I gaze out the window I broke through a brick wall with words. I can see nothing that happens anywhere but everything I need to thrive. Forbidden apples fall upward in serpentine lines of animosity and charm. I will never stop stopping. I belong here, where I cannot not appear.

EXPERIMENTAL LIFE

QUEER POEM

I'm

sad

about

my

ability

to

do

experimental

life

that

persists

beyond

this

post

yesterday

before

the

word

came

out

of

exclaiming

hello

we're

here

we're

sad

about

our

ability

to

do

much

hashtag

better

than

ink

beyond

pecs

beside

makeup

singing

in

a

bed

of

left

markup

that

all

messier

cries

not

alone

behind

above

against

along

among

inside

THE BAROMETER IN MY NECK

I love this scroll bar, increasing in density

your paw on my shoulder a gentle, foggy

offering. Meanwhile, I'm hunched

against some crooked shoulder-length wall tones

trying to determine how Leigh

Bowery can see out from inside that full immersion

wig. In the Bowery, there's this cobbled

Salvador Dali, leathery together

but then suddenly this moat appears

around my voice. You should come over,

you should try to be my cobbled life

says the worn-away toe of the boot, as it turns

back into a Lucky nightclub. "If we'd stayed there

two minutes longer, you'd have been the filling

in a sandwich." In this poem, I'm spread all

over town. I'm reaching toward the rough-

smooth line of your chin, a polluted creek, a non-

elegiac context without piazzas dangling

from the scenery. You can take another's voice,

and mock their lack, but Dalí will get it back.

BOBADYLLO*

The reporter poses a question:
We're sitting beneath a translucent shell that's
suddenly lifted, to reveal a guilt furnace
internecine arras. Mobius shadows
we let down our locks within
circle children, reduced to them, canvassing
the murk I am delivering to you, kilts and curls,
the damages or dampers we enlist.
Everything courts dusk, doodlee doodlee doodlee
doo — even the prescient chorus
who handles our introductory rate
encroached upon the plaza with cardboard signs.
The mistaken idea of the glamor in the
protest that hurts us, affirms this.
Consistently attached like a decal at the site,
a passive persistence of activism tongues
can pry lids. Yet somewhere a fist is pumped
for information, punishing the documentary film
and the gown that surrounds it, the oxygen.

My pronunciation of Bob Dylan's name as a small child

WIG CAP

Last week I was at the bookstore picking up Spinoza and Whitehead. That's an example of metonymy.

Spinoza and Whitehead wanted to go for a drink afterward but I said we should be getting home soon, I only have five hours before I turn into a pumpkin.

I handed the books over to the person at the counter to pay for them, and I said "it was a relief to find these; they are exactly what I needed." She said "So, where do you teach?"

Pumpkins are more frequent in the window displays. You and I form a figure in which the area of likeness and the area of unlikeness becomes thinner than a wig cap.

Sometime around then, I had a horrifying dream in which I was swallowing large rats while trying not to kill them.

I felt secure in the knowledge that my courageously humane rat-swallowing would not go unnoticed. A wig cap protects you from another's scalp disease.

I carved a bust of Spinoza on my pumpkin, and the costumed kids passed by the porch like an ostrich.

Friends had been calling; I cooked dinner that night in the last clean pot.

BERLIN

You know, a scene from Berlin lost about a thousand dollars in between halfsies. This is character development and earnest accompaniment of my hidden flower. Decorous, employment, filibuster, a light paraphernalia of jumbo terrycloth favors. Salt bomb in the midst of pointing your toes at the sea. Or my toes, that's a humbling Farrah impression. Dented mahogany pillow, I've been sitting up all night and clasping you between the realization Deb enforced. Politely, traveling westward with two cans as purposeful as a dynamic oh partial umbrella retort. I'm not making any cases for stereo-archetypal specialization, but I want to tag you. There, a battlecap of the sere and broadway. Time alters, penned a lung green allegory. On the cherry white map of bacon spats, intelligible felt hand design ringlet. Parity puss. Gyno poem-blocker stilt listening up the lint barrier of sound makeup. Gorge fetal air-conditioning peat nose. Commercial petting zilch. Tumble over a friend hill, perfect each loader second. I'm only partially aware of Sean. If it were pall-driven, lurid done cousin appropriate. Alt-sympatico linguist remorse, I wish I could swallow it. Endure it, I mean. Temporary eel filter comprising paramour linkage strength. Um, I'll just have a direction we came from? Park alternate roads for the cars and chalk, but baby if you want a dalliance quell short water break. Loquacious, I mean how loquacious of any real senator, to be so rudely interrupted by murk. Pal of a few short hours ago, unlend. Parted stimulus. The reason we became friends some desk magnet odor detective. Representing you, I'm totally French.

MOVEABLE TYPE

Let me recast these words in a different font
Mental typography could mean, to strike, to punch
I may be ubiquitous; I don't know what I want

To write is to be written molds screw-type taunt
Found your bumper-sticker marked down in the crying wolf shop
Let me recast these words in a different font

The more I confess, the more my post-Fordist rent
rises, gut response shifts from empathize to hunt
You may be ubiquitous; you don't know what you want

Watch your back alloy ally type-casting type-setting feint,
we pour hot metal into one Parnassus, then you're all like
let me recast these words in a different font

Downward pressure makes an even print
The hotel room drawer says, another you in a minute
I may be ubiquitous; I don't know what I want

We interrupt your tussle here: hey guys break it up, a glint
in the corner of our apostrophe enforcer passive tin emulsion
Let me recast these words in a different font
You may be ubiquitous; you don't know what you want.

THE BLUR

BOUQUET

"So, how are the kids?" They are suffering from their lack of existence, in the park, chasing a kite or morphing into mobius-strip-like shapes of language mesh, it's scary how a zoo can make you feel safe. We like to elide into the crowd, the mass, the prow of the boat cutting through the echo of the snowglobe, keeping an appointment and bereft of the appropriate fork. Instead we've developed a new, all-purpose utensil that incorporates every angle, a Picasso painting of a utensil, which though slightly tortured-looking and sometimes beaten up on the street, is nevertheless parking transgressively in your spot when you're not looking. Here's a gesture only an entitled punchbowl hand can make, we attempt while leaning over the banister to carouse with people who make half a million, then go home and hide, the syntactical confusion crooning us into velvet sheets of the poem. As long as we could hide, internalized normative surveillance coming over for a little red wine and some brie cheese in the evening, we'd catch the bouquet before knowing what it meant.

HYDRO-POWERED TURBINES

We spend all afternoon reading impenetrable texts like mystical objects, and when we look up the sun is ailing. It has been given too much meaning and it burns through us, so lazy and retrofitted with memory. To be open when we wish to survey and be surveilled, that is the best case scenario. A best case scenario is a tactical move, analyzing the situation for its strengths and weaknesses. A stream of consciousness winds its way through the volley of selves below in the street sprung with gardens at the edges. Hydro-powered turbines start up, initiated by a single mouse click, a roving self-formation. To humanize it, we encounter a sprig of rhythm, jutting out of the wall we thought solid, undermining it. We implies a tour through lands of delight as well as suffering, and a distance from that morning. From the bird's eye view out the roving window, a study in grey and faded tones. An absolute grid or relative grids are suggested but not definite, as we can step away from the shutters on our route to the kitchen for a cup of tea with purple antioxidants. Carving the notice onto a playful scrim, a trade off, and then erasing it, we rebound from intimacy into a bone enclosure.

NOCTURNE

Progress is overrated, if by progress we recall a lonely cyclist on a road dreaming of a mid-life crisis Aston Martin. Hello, cyclist. Hello, direct swathe of imperiled sky. Temp workers glide by the destabilized progress report of confidence, immanent sense. From where I stood by the endless bar, I could tell the rest of the war pack there I was in pain. We stood by in pain at the frondless air. To be meek, to sight under the tamped down light, lunging toward a treat. Don't shake hands with your landlord, shake your multicolored arms, bound chests, bound bodies in trouble which did that to themselves. To take pride in a barracuda well done, I'm falling into lyceum greens. Oh grass, handle my denial responsibly, with a soft hand just inches above cables, I-beams, circuits in the meat. With a soft hand that doesn't float around the room, but lands astray. I'm stumbling into the doorway of my residence, pushing out the air.

DRONES

A pigeon flies in an arcing spiral reminiscent of a more important bird to list on one's resume. We installed the screens to prevent disease. A resume is the involved house we remember to clean, hunkering beneath one's profile while dusting the near edge of the bookshelf, of an instep seam. I look back and it's not a pigeon, it's a risk. A profile is an image of ill birds gathering at the cornice of a nearby building—we anticipate food, a nest, or a peek in the full-length pigeon-mirror of others. Gradually it becomes clear that for a while now acid rain has been falling into our cup, a drop by drop which internally grows and rankles. We are becoming drones, we hear ourselves breaking the sound barrier overhead, we fear our best or worst qualities switching hats. In the light beneath the canteen sign we glimpsed the sheriff and the outlaw embracing, talking about us behind our horse in lush vocals slung back. To list is to enfold a new norm—that's what the outlaw spawns. An illustration of smoke on a defunct chimney. Drone smoke. From the roofline's edge you can see the route where we first rode into town, greeted by gasps of closure. Unite the rats of the air.

WITH A PETROLEUM COATING

The exoskeleton dries by the radiator. What is the usefulness of shells, as in putting them up to one's ear to detect the poem? Isn't it infringeable that we carry our mating rituals into teleology? Isn't it lately that our mates don't often insert parts? The problem, as if splashed onto canvas in a never-drying medium, isn't it that we can be hurt from without as if by wifi, by rumor? By cell tower? By stork? Thanks for caring. The storks along the beach stand on one leg, and then slowly generously fly away, including me, like a teacher who warns against trying to make absent things present. What do all these little knobs on the console do? This one flies us straight into battle with a petroleum coating. This one parodies the last erotic feeling. This one entices us to have babies with the reader, sitting lax on a conveyor belt that suddenly falls off at the end into someplace decent. In your guest room, draped with necklaces, we feel thinner than a Mobius strip, real wolf fur rug inside and out, real antler chandelier. In your guest room we peel an alien tangerine.

WALKING UP TO THE PUNCHBOWL AS IF YOU OWN IT

Gurus don't throw hissyfits. For the rest, a long entourage leads practically out of town, awaiting the enlightenment cue of "Guru, party of two?" We like to amaze ourselves, inly, e-place, farming out our better part to someone who prevents us re-entering meatspace. If masochism is truly the only subject position, we could always just stay home and complain about our own cooking. Oh, the beets don't taste right, oh the spinach has wilted again after being held too long against the flame. To flame is to generate hotness, a carbon-based kaleidoscope meddling with propriety. What is this, beet juice? Bot kiss? A guru and a recently evolved fish with legs walk into a bar. Here's a punchline only a kool-aid intoxicated critic would make: I am leaving you out of the invitation to the entourage, which was so juicy and cold, but it's ok because there's a kind of social blurring which emerges between understandability and the sex you want to be accepted as. As if my own eye weren't an unfolding platform I could make you walk too. The blur that was you late at night hunkered down watching gurus necking in your brother's beat-up car, the back seat bouncing up and down guru-style. The good news is we've discovered a breakthrough, in our business and yours, to evoke and encourage hotness, churning out double the expected sales through just a few words on the label: "rinse, repeat." Wait, why are you leaving? The guru is you.

ACKNOWLEDGEMENTS

Thanks to the editors of all journals and anthologies in which these poems previously appeared: "After Before And After" at *PBS Newshour* (online), in *The Brooklyn Rail* (online), and in the print anthologies *The Best American Experimental Writing 2016* (Wesleyan University Press) and *More Truly and More Strange: 100 Contemporary American Self-Portrait Poems* (Persea Books). "The Valleys Are So Lush and Steep" was published at *The Academy of American Poets* (Poets.org) online and in the anthology *Super Gay Poems: LGBTQIA+ Poetry after Stonewall* (Harvard University Press). "No One Could See The Vast Crowd" appeared in *Boston Review* (online). "Everyone Is a Little Trans" was published at *PEN America* (online). "Identification" was published in *Cream City Review's* "GenreQueer Feature." "Violet Speech" first appeared as a limited edition 24-page print chapbook from Second Avenue Poetry, and sections from it also previously appeared in the journal *Spiral Orb* (online) and the anthology *Readings in Contemporary Poetry: An Anthology* (Dia Art Center / Yale University Press). "Exclusively on Venus" was published at *The Academy of American Poets* and in *The Brooklyn Rail*. (both online). "Canyon of Heroines" also appeared at *The Academy of American Poets* online. "Pussy" and "Queer Poem" were published in *Michigan Quarterly Review's MQR Mixtape* (online). "Make a Wish" appeared in *Interim Poetry and Poetics* online. "Permanently" was published in *Posit* (online). "The Barometer in My Neck" appeared on *The Poetry Project's* website. "Bobadyllo" was published in the print journal *Aufgabe*. "Wig Cap" appeared in the print journal *Sonora Review*. "Moveable Type" was written as part of the Oulipo art exhibition *Pattern Variants* (AC Institute, NY). "Bouquet," "Hydro-Powered Turbines," and "Nocturne" appeared in *Eratio* (online). "Drones" was published in *The Arts Fuse* (online), *Texas Review* (print), and the anthology *Devouring the Green: Fear of a Human Planet* (Jaded Ibis Press). "With a Petroleum

Coating" appeared in *Vanitas* (print) and in *The Academy of American Poets' Poem-A-Day* online. And "Walking Up to the Punchbowl As If You Own It" appeared in the print journal *Vanitas*.

A special thanks to everyone who helped this book come into being over the past decade and a half, especially those who read drafts of the final manuscript carefully and offered useful comments: Charles Alexander, Nicholas Birns, Helen Bronston, Janet Holmes, Katie Peterson, Norman Fischer, Sarah Riggs, Stephanie Burt, Tenney Nathanson, and Samuel Ace. Thanks to Timothy Liu, Roberto Tejada, and the Saturnalia Books Staff for selecting this book for the Alma Award. And thanks to graphic designer Robin Vuchnich for a beautiful book design.

Thanks also to those who read and responded to individual poems in memorable or productive ways, including Akilah Oliver, Andrew Levy, Anne Waldman, Anselm Berrigan, Aurora Mattia, Avren Keating, Barbara Cully, BK Fischer, Bonnie Reid, Buzz Slutzky, Camille Roy, Carol Mirakove, Carolyn Hembree, Charles Bernstein, Ching-In Chen, Claudia Keelan, Dan Healy, David Kellogg, Donna de la Perriere, E. Tracy Grinnell, Eero Talo, Efrain Gonzalez, Eileen Myles, Emily Skillings, Eric Magraine, Erin Lynn, Eve Kosofsky Sedgwick, Evelyn Reilly, Everett Maroon, Filip Marinovich, Gregory Vincent St Thomasino, Hal Sedgwick, Hannah Romito, James Sherry, Jamila Wimberly, Jason Schneiderman, Jen Benka, Jimena Lucero, Jesse Seldess, Joel Lewis, Joel Sloman, Kimberly Lyons, John Godfrey, John Mulrooney, Joseph Lease, Joy Ladin, Julian Brolaski, Julie Choffel, Karen Schiff, Kyle Dacuyan, Lee Ann Brown, Lin Peterson, Lonely Christopher, Maria Damon, Mark Weiss, Marthe Reed, Matvei Yankelevich, Max Wolf Valerio, Meg Day, Melissa Buckheit,

Michael Lally, Michael Weinstein, Natasha Dennerstein, Nathaniel Siegel, Nicole Wallace, Nita Noveno, Pam Dick, Patricia Peterson, Paul Legault, Rachel Hadas, Regie Cabico, Richard Peterson, Ryan Schulte, Ruth Lepson, Sam Witt, Samuel Ace, Sarah Sarai, Scott Campbell, Sean Cole, Stefania Heim, Steve Dickison, Steven F. Kruger, Susan Lewis, Susan Rudy, Suzanne Wise, Taylor Brady, TC Tolbert, Timothy Donnelly, Thomas Fink, Tracie Morris, Trish Salah, Vincent Katz, Wayne Koestenbaum, and everyone at the Boston Poetry Marathon.

ABOUT TRACE PETERSON

Trace Kelsey Peterson was born in Connecticut in 1978. Peterson is a poet, editor, and literary scholar. She is the author of two books of poems: *Since I Moved In* which won the Gil Ott Award from Chax Press, and *The Valleys Are So Lush and Steep*, which won the Alma Book Award from Saturnalia Books. She has also authored numerous chapbooks of poems, including *Cumulus* (Portable Press at Yo-Yo Labs) and *Violet Speech* (Second Avenue Poetry). Peterson is co-editor (with TC Tolbert) of the ground-breaking anthology *Troubling the Line: Trans and Genderqueer Poetry and Poetics* (Nightboat Books) and also co-editor (with Eli Goldblatt and Gregory Laynor) of *Arrive on Wave: Collected Poems of Gil Ott* (Chax Press). She edits the journal/small press *EOAGH* which has won 2 Lambda Literary Awards (including the first given in Transgender Poetry) and a National Jewish Book Award for Poetry. Peterson's poems have recently appeared in *Super Gay Poems: LGBTQIA+ Poetry after Stonewall* (Harvard University Press), *Interim Poetry & Poetics*, *The Arts Fuse*, Michigan Quarterly Review's *MQR Mixtape*, *More Truly and More Strange: 100 Contemporary American Self-Portrait Poems* (Persea Books), *The Academy of American Poets Poem-A-Day*, and *Boston Review*. Her criticism and scholarly writing have appeared in *Seeking Our Places: Innovations in Creative Writing Research, Methodologies, and Practices* (Peter Lang Publishing), *The Weird Sister Collection* (The Feminist Press), *A Companion to American Poetry* (Wiley Blackwell), *The SAGE Encyclopedia of Trans Studies* (SAGE Publications), *TSQ: Transgender Studies Quarterly*, and numerous edited collections. Peterson holds a PhD in English from The Graduate Center, CUNY, an MFA in Creative Writing from the University of Arizona, and a BA from Wesleyan University. As a professor, she has taught at Yale University, Naropa University's Summer Writing Program, The Poetry Project at St Marks, Parsons School of Design, Hunter College, and other schools in the CUNY System. Previously the 2021-2022 N.E.H Post-Doctoral Fellow in Poetics at Emory University's Fox Center, Peterson has most recently been a Visiting Assistant Professor at the University of Connecticut.

Also by Trace Peterson

Since I Moved In

Troubling the Line: Trans and Genderqueer Poetry and Poetics
(co-edited with TC Tolbert)

Arrive on Wave: Collected Poems of Gil Ott
(co-edited with Eli Goldblatt and Gregory Laynor)

The Valleys Are So Lush and Steep was printed in Palatino
www.saturnaliabooks.org

www.ingramcontent.com/pod-product-compliance
Lightning Source LLC
Chambersburg PA
CBHW081459070526
44586CB00019B/2424